MW01609462

EDUCATION AND THE GROWING CHILD

EDUCATION AND
THE GROWING CHILD

SRI AUROBINDO INSTITUTE
OF RESEARCH IN SOCIAL SCIENCES
SRI AUROBINDO SOCIETY
PONDICHERRY

First Edition: 1974
Second Revised Edition: 1996
Reprinted: 2002

Compiled and Edited by
Prof. Norman C. Dowsett
Prof. Sita Ram Jayaswal
M. S. Srinivasan
Vijay

Rs. 35.00
ISBN 81-7060-101-0
Website: www.sriaurobindosociety.org.in

Published by:
Sri Aurobindo Institute of Research in Social Sciences
A Unit of Sri Aurobindo Society, Pondicherry
Printed at Sri Aurobindo Ashram Press, Pondicherry
Printed in India

CONTENTS

CONTENTS

Preface

Some of the important developments in modern thought are the new, positive and liberal ideas emerging in the field of child education. We have come a long way in this field from the orthodox barbarous ideas of hammering the child into fixed moulds according to the preconceived prejudices of the teacher or the parent, to the infinitely more liberal ideals of modern times bringing to the school fresh air in which the child can breathe in an atmosphere of freedom, joy, understanding and love.

But even in these new approaches to education – which are of course in the right direction – there are many aspects and problems of child education which remain unsolved. For example we often do not seem to have any clear vision of what are the goals of child education. Some crucial questions like what are the various faculties to be developed in a child and how to develop them, and the problem of manifesting the higher nature of the child through his moral, aesthetic and spiritual powers are not given sufficient attention. The new thought in education is unanimous in upholding the value of freedom in the education of the child. But how to educate the child to make the right use of freedom for his own higher evolution and progress is a crucial problem of child education which has still not been solved completely.

The solution to all these problems requires a new psychology and a new vision of the child and man. One of the major inadequacies of modern thought is the lack of sufficient psychological knowledge, experience and understanding of the spiritual dimension of man which is the source of all his psychological energies. Modern psychology tries to probe into the laws and processes of the conscious and subconscious life of man, but without a clear understanding of the laws and truths of the inner and higher origins of man's actions. But it is only in the spiritual dimension of man that can be found the secret of true harmony and integration.

Here lies the importance of Sri Aurobindo and the Mother's integral spiritual vision of education. They have given to the world an integral system of education which is based on the eternal truths of man's aspiration for perfection and progress. It is a completely new psychology applied to the education of the whole man and for the whole of life.

Based on this new vision and approach, the education of the child must begin even before his birth. It must progress from the prenatal stage through modern concepts of playschool and kindergarten, through the psychological phases of adolescence where the physical mind has to be disciplined and assured of security and love, where the vital and emotional mind has to fulfil itself by self-expression through all art forms and manifestations of beauty and harmony, to where the thinking mind has to be given the freedom to discover for itself the world of science and the mental forms of the universe, and finally to the stage in which all of them become the instruments of the spirit within.

The articles in this volume of the "Integral Education Series" emphasise the integral approach to child education which has such deep roots in the expanding life of today. We are grateful to the authors and publishers of the articles presented in this volume. We specially acknowledge the contributions of Prof. Norman Dowsett and Prof. S.R. Jayaswal who edited the first edition which was published in 1974. This second edition has been greatly revised and enlarged.

Education of the Child

SRI AUROBINDO

Formerly, education was merely a mechanical forcing of the child's nature into arbitrary grooves of training and knowledge in which his individual subjectivity was the last thing considered, and his family upbringing was a constant repression and compulsory shaping of his habits, his thoughts, his character into the mould fixed for them by the conventional ideas or individual interests and ideals of the teachers and parents. The discovery that education must be a bringing out of the child's own intellectual and moral capacities to their highest possible value and must be based on the psychology of the child-nature was a step forward towards a more healthy because a more sub- jective system; but it still fell short because it still regarded him as an object to be handled and moulded by the teacher, to be educated. But at least there was a glimmer- ing of the realisation that each human being is a self- developing soul and that the business of both parent and teacher is to enable and to help the child to educate himself, to develop his own intellectual, moral, aesthetic and practical capacities and to grow freely as an organic being, not to be kneaded and pressured into form like an inert plastic material. It is not yet realised what this soul is or that the true secret, whether with child or man, is to help him to find his deeper self, the real psychic entity within. That, if we ever give it a chance to come forward, and still more if we call it into the foreground as "the

1

leader of the march set in our front," will itself take up most of the business of education out of our hands and develop the capacity of the psychological being towards a realisation of its potentialities of which our present mechanical view of life and man and external routine methods of dealing with them prevent us from having any experience or forming any conception. These new educational methods are on the straight way to this truer dealing. The closer touch attempted with the psychical entity behind the vital and physical mentality and an increasing reliance on its possibilities must lead to the ultimate discovery that man is inwardly a soul and a conscious power of the Divine and that the evocation of this real man within is the right object of education and indeed of all human life if it would find and live according to the hidden Truth and deepest law of its own being.

*

A child of seven or eight, and that is the earliest permissible age for the commencement of any regular kind of study, is capable of a good deal of concentration if he is interested. Interest is, after all, the basis of concentration. We make his lessons supremely uninteresting and repellent to the child, a harsh compulsion the basis of teaching and then complain of his restless inattention! The substitution of a natural self-education by the child for the present unnatural system will remove this objection of inability. A child, like a man, if he is interested, much prefers to get to the end of his subject rather than leave it unfinished. To lead him on step by step, interesting and absorbing him in each as it comes, until he has mastered his subject is the true art of teaching.

2

The first attention of the teacher must be given to the medium and the instruments, and, until these are perfected, to multiply subjects of regular instruction is to waste time and energy. When the mental isntruments are sufficiently developed to acquire a language easily and swiftly, that is the time to introduce him to many languages, not when he can only partially understand what he is taught and masters it laboriously and imperfectly. Moreover, one who has mastered his own language, has one very necessary facility for mastering another. With the linguistic faculty unsatisfactorily developed in one's own tongue, to master others is impossible. To study science with the faculties of observation, judgment, reasoning and comparison only slightly developed is to undertake a useless and thankless labour. So it is with all other subjects.

The mother-tongue is the proper medium of education and therefore the first energies of the child should be directed to the thorough mastering of the medium. Almost every child has an imagination, an instinct for words, a dramatic faculty, a wealth of idea and fancy. These should be interested in the literature and history of the nation. Instead of stupid and dry spelling and reading books, looked on as a dreary and ungrateful task, he should be introduced by rapidly progressive stages to the most interesting parts of his own literature and the life around him and behind him, and they should be put before him in such a way as to attract and appeal to the qualities of which I have spoken. All other study at this period should be devoted to the perfection of the mental functions and the moral character. A foundation should be laid at this time for the study of history, science, philosophy, art, but not in an obtrusive and formal manner. Every child is a lover of interesting narrative, a hero-worhipper and a patriot. Appeal to these qualities in him and through them let him master without knowing it the living and human parts of his nation's history. Every child is an inquirer, an investigator, analyser, a merciless anatomist. Appeal to those qualities in him and let him acquire without knowing it the right temper and the necessary fundamental knowledge of the scientist. Every child has an insatiable intellectual curiosity and turn for metaphysical enquiry. Use it to draw him on slowly to an understanding of the world and himself. Every child has the gift of imitation and a touch of imaginative power. Use it to give him the groundwork of the faculty of the artist.

It is by allowing Nature to work that we get the benefit of the gifts she has bestowed on us. Humanity in its education of children has chosen to thwart and hamper her processes and, by so doing, has done much to thwart and hamper the rapidity of its onward march. Happily, saner ideas are now beginning to prevail. But the way has not yet been found. The past hangs about our necks with all its prejudices and errors and will not leave us; it enters into our most radical attempts to return to the guidance of the all-wise Mother. We must have the courage to take up clearer knowledge and apply it fearlessly in the interests of posterity. Teaching by snippets must be relegated to the lumber-room of dead sorrows. The first work is to interest the child in life, work and knowledge, to develop his instruments of knowledge with the utmost thoroughness, to give him mastery of the medium he must use. Afterwards, the rapidity with which he will learn will make up for any delay in taking up regular studies, and it will be found that, where now he learns a few things badly, then he will learn many things thoroughly well.

*

The first qualities of the mind that have to be developed are those which can be grouped under observation. We notice some things, ignore others. Even of what we notice, we observe very little. A general perception of an object is what we all usually carry away from a cursory half-attentive glance. A closer attention fixes its place, form, nature as distinct from its surroundigs. Full concentration of the faculty of observation gives us all the knowledge that the three chief senses can gather about the object, or if we touch or taste, we may gather all that the five senses can tell of its nature and properties. Those who make use of the sixth sense, the poet, the painter, the Yogin, can also gather much that is hidden from the ordinary observer. The scientist by investigation ascertains other facts open to a minuter observation. These are the components of the faculty of observation, and it is obvious that its basis is attention, which may be only close or close and minute. We may gather much even from a passing glance at an object, if we have the habit of concentrating the attention and the habit of sattwic receptivity. The first thing the teacher has to do is to accustom the pupil to concentrate attention.

We may take the instance of a flower. Instead of looking casually at it and getting a casual impression of scent, form and colour, he should be encouraged to know the flower – to fix in his mind the exact shade, the peculiar glow, the precise intensity of the scent, the beauty of curve and design in the form. His touch should assure itself of the texture and its peculiarities. Next, the flower should be taken to pieces and its structure examined with the same carefulness of observation. All this should be done not as a task, but as an object of interest by skilfully arranged questions suited to the learner which will draw him on to observe and investigate one thing after the other until he has almost unconsciously mastered the whole.

Memory and judgment are the next qualities that will be called upon, and they should be encouraged in the same unconscious way. The student should not be made to repeat the same lesson over again in order to remember it. That is a mechanical, burdensome and unintelligent way of training the memory. A similar but different flower should be put in the hands and he should be encouraged to note it with the same care, but with the avowed object of noting the similarities and differences. By this practice daily repeated the memory will naturally be trained. Not only so, but the mental centres of comparison and contrast will be developed. The learner will begin to observe as a habit the similarities of things and their differences. The teacher should take every care to encourage the perfect growth of this faculty and habit. At the same time, the laws of species and genus will begin to dawn on the mind and, by a skilful following and leading of the young developing mind, the scientific habit, the scientific attitude and the fundamental facts of scientific knowledge may in a very short time be made part of its permanent equipment. The observation and comparison of flowers, leaves, plants, trees will lay the foundations of botanical knowledge without loading the mind with names and that dry set acquisition of informations which is the beginning of cramming and detested by the healthy human mind when it is fresh from nature and unspoiled by unnatural

6

habits. In the same way by the observation of the stars, astronomy, by the observation of earth, stones, etc., geology, by the observation of insects and animals, entomology and zoology may be founded. A little later chemistry may be started by interesting observation of experiments without any formal teaching or heaping on the mind of formulas and book knowledge. There is no scientific subject the perfect and natural mastery of which cannot be prepared in early childhood by this training of the faculties to observe, compare, remember and judge various classes of objects. It can be done easily and attended with a supreme and absorbing interest in the mind of the student. Once the taste is created, the boy can be trusted to follow it up with all the enthusiasm of youth in his leisure hours. This will prevent the necessity at a later age of teaching him everything in class.

*

As in the education of the mind, so in the education of the heart, the best way is to put the child into the right road to his own perfection and encourage him to follow it, watching, suggesting, helping, but not interfering. The one excellent element in the English boarding school is that the master at his best stands there as a moral guide and example, leaving the boys largely to influence and help each other in following the path silently shown to them. But the method practised is crude and marred by the excess of outer discipline, for which the pupils have no respect except that of fear and the exiguity of the inner assistance. The little good that is done is outweighed by much evil. The old Indian system of the *guru* commanding by his knowledge and sanctity the implicit obedience, perfect admiration, reverent emulation of the student was a far superior method of moral discipline. It is impossible to restore that ancient system; but it is not impossible to substitute the wise friend, guide and helper for the hired instructor or the benevolent policeman which is all that the European system usually makes of the pedagogue.

The first rule of moral training is to suggest and invite, not command or impose. The best method of suggestion is by personal example, daily converse and the books read from day to day. These books should contain, for the younger student, the lofty examples of the past given, not as moral lessons, but as things of supreme human interest, and, for the elder student, the great thoughts of great souls, the passages of literature which set fire to the highest emotions and prompt the highest ideals and aspirations, the records of history and biography which exemplify the living of those great thoughts, noble emotions and aspiring ideals. This is a kind of good company, *satsanga*, which can seldom fail to have effect so long as sententious sermonising is avoided, and becoems of the highest effect if the personal life of the teacher is itself moulded by the great things he places before his pupils. It cannot, however, have full force unless the young life is given an opportunity, within its limited sphere, of embodying in action the moral impulses which rise within it. The thirst of knowledge, the self-devotion, the purity, the renunciation of the Brahmin, – the courage, ardour, honour, nobility, chivalry, patriotism of the Kshatriya, – the beneficence, skill, industry, generous enterprise and large open-handedness of the Vaisya, – the self-effacement and loving service of the Sudra, – these are the qualities of the Aryan. They constitute the moral temper

8

we desire in our young men, in the whole nation. But how can we get them if we do not give opportunities to the young to train themselves in the Aryan tradition, to form by the practice and familiarity of childhood and boyhood the stuff of which their adult lives must be made?

Every boy should, therefore, be given practical opportunity as well as intellectual encouragement to develop all that is best in the nature. If he has bad qualities, bad habits, bad *saṁskāras* whether of mind or body, he should not be treated harshly as a delinquent, but encouraged to get rid of them by the Rajayogic method of *saṁyama*, rejection and substitution. He should be encouraged to think of them, not as sins or offences, but as symptoms of a curable disease, alterable by a steady and sustained effort of the will, – falsehood being rejected whenever it rises into the mind and replaced by truth, fear by courage, selfishness by sacrifice and renunciation, malice by love. Great care will have to be taken that unformed virtues are not rejected as faults. The wildness and recklessness of many young natures are only the overflowings of an excessive strength, greatness and nobility. They should be purified, not discouraged.

Teaching Children

THE MOTHER

It would be interesting to formualte or to work out a new method of teaching children; to take them very small, very small, it is easy. One will need people (Oh, one will need very remarkable professors), who have first, a sufficient documentation of what they know, to be able to answer all questions; and, at the same time, at least the knowledge if not the experience (the experience would be better) of the true intellectual and intuitive attitude (and naturally, the capacity would be still preferable), but in any case, the knowledge that the true way of knowledge is through the mental silence – a silence that is wide-awake, turned towards the most true Consciousness, and the capacity to receive what comes from there. The best would be to have this capacity; in any case, it should be explained that this is the true thing, a kind of demonstration, that it works not only from the point of view of what should be learned, of the whole field of knowledge, but also of the entire field of all that should be done, the capacity to receive the exact indication of how to do it; and as one advances, changes into a very clear perception of what should be done, and a precise indication of when it should be done. At the very least, the children, as soon as they have the capacity to think (it begins at 7 years but towards 14 years it is very clear) should be given small indications at 7 and a complete explanation at 14, of how to do it, and that it is the unique method to enter into relation with the profound truth of things, that all the rest is a mental approximation, more or less inapt of something that can be known directly.

The conclusion is that the professors must themselves have at least a sincere beginning of discipline and experience; it is not a matter of collecting books and retelling them like that: one cannot be a professor, like this. The whole world is like this, one has only to let the outside world be as it is if it gives it pleasure. We here are not propagandists; we simply want to show what can be done, and try to prove that it must be done.

When one has very small children, it is marvellous. There, there are so few things to do: it is sufficient *to be*.

> Never to deceive oneself.
> Never to be angry.
> Always to be understanding.

And to understand and see clearly why there was this movement, why this impulsion, what is the interior constitution of the child, what one should fortify and put in front. There is only this to be done and then to leave them, to leave them free to blossom, to give them only the occasion to see many things, to touch many things, to do as many things as possible. It is very amusing. And above all, never to try and impose on them what one believes one knows.

Never to scold. Always to understand, and if the child is capable, to explain; if he is incapable for an explanation (if one is oneself capable of it) to replace the false vibvration with a true one.... But this... this is to ask of the teachers a perfection which they rarely have.

11

But it would be very interesting to make a programme for the professors and the true programme of studies, right from below, which is so plastic and which receives impressions so deeply. If one could give them some drops of truth when they are very young, it would blossom out naturally as the being grew. It would be a beautiful work.

*

There is another quality which must be cultivated in the child even when it is quite young. It is the feeling of unease, of a lack of moral poise which he has when he does certain things, not because he has been told not to do such things nor because he is afraid of being punished, but spontaneously. For example, a child who hurts a comrade of his by his mischief, if he is in his normal, natural state will feel a discomfort, a sorrow within his being, because what he has done is contrary to his inner truth.

For in spite of all instruction, in spite of all that thought can think of, there is something within that has the feeling of a perfection, of a higher status, of a truth which unfortunately is contradicted by all movements contrary to that truth. If the child is not corrupted because of his environment, because of deplorable examples that surround him, that is to say, if he remains in his normal, spontaneous condition, without anyone telling him anything whatsoever, he will feel a discomfort when he does something which contradicts the truth of his being. And it is just there that is to be based, later on, his effort for progress....

There is only one true guide, the inner guide, who does not pass through the mental consciousness.

Naturally, if a child receives a disastrous education, he

will try more and more to extinguish in him this small true thing and at times he succeeds so well in doing it that he loses all contact with it and also the power to distinguish good from evil. That is why I insist on that and I say that from the very earliest age children must be taught that there is a reality within – within themselves, within the earth, within the universe and that himself, the earth and the universe exist only as a function of this truth and if it did not exist, he would not last, even the short time he lasts and that everything would dissolve as soon as it is created. And because that is the efficient basis of the universe, naturally it is that which will triumph, and all which contradicts that cannot be as enduring, because it is That, the eternal thing which is at the basis of the universe.

This does not mean naturally that one should give a child philosophical explanations, but one can very well give him the feeling of a kind of inner ease, satisfaction and at times an intense joy when he obeys this little thing very silent which is within him, which will prevent him from doing what is contradictory to it. It is upon an experience of this kind that the teaching should be based. One must give the child the impression that nothing can last unless he has within him this true satisfaction which alone is durable....

To give theories to children serves absolutely no purpose, for as soon as the mind will wake up, he will find a thousand reasons to contradict your theories and he will be right....

If you were an experienced observer, if you could take note of what happens in a being, simply by looking at his eyes!... It is said the eye is the mirror of the soul; it is a

13

popular way of speaking, but if the eyes do not express the psychic, the reason is that it is very much behind, veiled by very many things; look at the eyes of the children with care and you will see a kind of light – people say candid – but so true, so true that looks at the world with wonder. Well, this wonder, it is the wonder of the psychic that sees the truth but does not understand much of the world, for it is too far from there. Children have that, but as they learn, become more intelligent, more educated, that thing fades away and you see in their eyes all kinds of things: thoughts, desires, passions, wickedness, but that kind of a small very pure flame is no more there. And you may be sure that it is the mind that has entered there and the psychic has gone very much behind.

Even in the case of a child who does not possess a sufficiently developed brain to understand, if you simply pass on to him a vibration of protection or affection or solicitude or consolation, you will see that he responds.

*

A rule to be strictly followed. It is *absolutely* forbidden to beat the children – a blow of any kind, even the simple little slap or the so-called friendly slap, is forbidden. To strike a child because it does not obey or understand or because it disturbs others is a sign of lack of self-control and it is as pernicious for the teacher as for the student.

*

Never scold a child. People reproach me that I speak ill of the parents. But I have seen them in action, and I know 90% of the parents snub a child who comes confessing spontaneously a fault: "You are nasty, get away, I am

14

busy" instead of hearing the child patiently, explaining to him in what lies the fault, how he should have acted. And the child who had come with a good disposition, goes back altogether hurt with the feeling: "Why am I treated in this way?" Then the child sees that the parents are not perfect – which is evidently the case at present – he sees that you are wrong and says to himself: "Why does he scold me!"

*

It is not with severity but with self-mastery that children are controlled.

*

One must never get angry in front of the children. They lose their respect for the teacher.

*

Another thing should be taught to a child from his early age; the taste for cleanliness and hygienic habits. But if you wish to get from the child this taste for cleanliness and respect for the rules of hygiene, you must take great care not to instil into him the fear of illness. Fear is the worst incentive for education and the surest way of attracting what is feared.

*

One must have a lot of patience with young children, and repeat the same thing to them several times, explaining it to them in various ways. It is only gradually that it enters their mind.

*

The teacher should not be a book that is read aloud, the same for everyone, no matter what his nature and character. The first duty of the teacher is to help the student to know himself and to discover what he is capable of doing.

For that one must observe his games, the activities to which he is drawn naturally and spontaneously and also what he likes to learn, whether his intelligence is awake, the stories he enjoys, the activities which interest him, the human achievements which attract him.

The teacher must find out the category to which each of the children in his care belongs. And if after careful observation he discovers two or three exceptional children who are eager to learn and who love progress, he should help them to make use of their energies for this purpose by giving them the freedom of choice that encourages individual growth.

The old method of the seated class to which the teacher gives the same lesson for all, is certainly economical and easy, but also very ineffective, and so time is wasted for everybody.

*

What you should do is to teach the children to take interest in what they are doing – that is not the same thing as interesting the students! You must arouse in them the desire for knowledge, for progress. One can take an interest in anything – in sweeping a room, for example – if one does it with concentration, in order to gain an experience, to make a progress, to become more conscious....

Most teachers want to have *good students*: students who are studious and attentive, who understand and know many things, who can answer well – good students. This spoils everything. The students begin to consult books, to study, to learn. Then they rely only on books, on what others say or write, and they lose contact with the superconscient part which receives knowledge by intuition. This contact often exists in a small child but it is lost in the course of his education.

For the students to be able to progress in the right direction, it is obvious that the teachers should have understood this and changed their old way of seeing and teaching. Without that, my work is at a standstill.

*

Children have everything to learn. This should be their main preoccupation in order to prepare themselves for a useful and productive life.

At the same time, as they grow up, they must discover in themselves the thing or things which interest them most and which they are capable of doing well. There are latent faculties to be developed. There are also faculties to be discovered.

Children must be taught to like to overcome difficulties, and also that this gives a special value to life; when one knows how to do it, it destroys boredom for ever and gives an altogether new interest to life.

We are on earth to progress and we have everything to learn.

*

In assessing the possibilities of a child, ordinary moral notions are not of much use. Natures that are rebellious, undisciplined, obstinate, often conceal qualities that no one has known how to use. Indolent natures may also

17

have a great potential for calm and patience.

*

It is a whole world to discover and easy solutions are not of much use. The teacher must be even more hard-working than the student in order to learn how to discern and bring out the best of their different characters.

*

Here's something then which already changes [for you teachers] your outlook on education completely.

Essentially, the *only thing* you should do assiduously is to teach them to know themselves and choose their own destiny, the path they will follow; to teach them to look at themselves, understand themselves *and* to will what they want to be. That is infinetely more important than teaching them what happened on earth in former times, or even how the earth is built, or even... indeed, all sorts of things which are quite a necessary grounding if you want to live the ordianry life in the world, for if you don't know them, anyone will immediately put you down intellectually: "Oh, he is an idiot, he knows nothing."

But still, at any age, if you [children] are studious and have the will to do it, you can also take up books and work; you don't need to go to school for that. There are enough books in the world to teach you things. There are even many more books than necessary....

But what is very important is to know what you want. And for this a minimum of freedom is necessary. You must not be under a compulsion or an obligation. You must be able to do things whole-heartedly. If you are lazy, well, you will know what it means to be lazy.... You

18

know, in life idlers are obliged to work ten times more than others, for what they do they do badly, so they are obliged to do it again. But these are things one must learn by experience. They can't be instilled into you.

*

It is very difficult to know how to organise one's own freedom oneself. Still, if you were to succeed in doing that, in giving yourself your own discipline – and for higher reasons, not in order to pass exams, to make a career, please your teachers, win many prizes, or all the ordinary reasons children have: in order not to be scolded, not to be punished, for all that; we leave out all those reasons – if you manage to impose a discipline upon yourself – each one his own, there is no need to follow someone else's – a discipline simply because you want to progress and draw the best out of yourself, then... Oh! you will be far superior to those who follow the ordinary school disciplines. That is what I wanted to try. Mind you, I don't say I have failed; I still have great hope that you will know how to profit by this unique opportunity. But all the same, there is something you must find out; it is the *necessity* of an inner discipline. Without discipline you won't be able to gët anywhere, without discipline you can't even live the normal life of a normal man. But instead of having the conventional discipline of ordinary societies or ordinary institutions, I would have liked and I still want you to have the discipline you set yourselves, for the love of perfection, your own perfection, the perfection of your being.

...And because I have a very marked aversion for conventional disciplines, social and others, it does not mean that you must abstain from all discipline. I would like everyone to find his own, in the sincerity of his inner aspiration and the will to realise himself.

And so, the aim of all those who know, whether they are teachers, instructors or any others, the very purpose of those who know, is to inform you, to help you. When you are in a situation which seems difficult to you, you put your problem and, from their personal experience, they can tell you, "No, it is like this or it is like that, and you must do this, you must try that." So, instead of forcing you to absorb theories, principles and so-called laws, and a more or less abstract knowledge, they would be there to give you information about things, from the most material to the most spiritual, each one within his own province and according to his capacity.

... That is the usefulness, the *true* usefulness of teachers and instructors. They have learnt more or less by practice or through a special study, and they can teach you those things it is indispensable to know. That makes you save time, a lot of time. But that is their only usefulness: to be able to answer questions. And, in fact, you should have a brain which is lively enough to ask questions.

*

Isn't this immense freedom we are given dangerous for those who are not yet awake, who are still unconscious? How can we account for this good fortune we have been given?

Danger and risk form part of all forward movement. Without them, nothing would ever move; besides, they are indispensable in forming the character of those who want to progress.

*

20

According to what I see and know, as a general rule, children over 14 should be allowed their independence and should be given advice only if and when they ask for it.

They should know that they are responsible for managing their own existence.

Children and Child Mentality

NOLINI KANTA GUPTA

Children are often found to be very cruel to animals. Why is it so? Their treatment of birds especially is notorious. To seek out nests and pull them down, to capture nestlings and put them to all kinds of torture, to pick up eggs and dash them to pieces are for children most interesting games. They seem to take particular delight in varying and enhancing as much as possible the torture they can inflict.

One reason that can be adduced for the callousness of a child's sensibility is his self-centredness: he is wholly himself, isolated from others, has not yet learnt the social needs and virtues. All he does and feels is for himself, for his own pleasure and free self-assertion. His growing individuality, in order to grow, cuts itself aloof from others and loses the sense of others having the same value as itself. Being self-regarding, to that extent he ceases to be other-regarding. Fellow-feeling is a sentiment that grows later on, as the result of shocks in mutual inter-change. Real sympathy is a movement of mature consciousness.

The inquisitiveness that so strongly possesses a child is also the drive of an awakening and growing consciousness. He indulges in breaking, tearing, ripping because of this curiosity, this keen edge of a developing and experimenting consciousness. It seems to be hard and unfeeling, even an aberration, precisely because of the egocentric nature of the child consciousness yet unfamiliar with

22

values normal to age and experience.

But if it is nature to a certain extent that makes the child so apathetic, self-regarding and cruel, it is not the only cause and it is not the whole story. There are other very active factors in life that affect and mould the child's consciousness from the very beginning.

The child, we can take, comes into the world with a more or less clean slate to record the reactions of life. In the early period he is still nearer his psychic being which is not yet thrown back or covered over by the impacts and impressions of the world. The first conscious contacts with the world are not generally happy for the child. He meets things all around that go against the grain of his still sensitive psychic consciousness.

The first quarrel he witnesses between his parents, the first rough behaviour or movement of an elder that shakes his attention, the first lie that he hears uttered by his teacher, act almost as shellshocks to his nerves. And as he grows, lessons like these are showered upon him from all sides and no wonder if his consciousness very soon gets warped and twisted, he too begins his own game in the line he observes and experiences.

Only, not being guided or controlled by reason and experience, he overdoes the thing, and because of his age, what in an adult is a matter of course, trivial and insignificant, looms large and ominous in his case. The surroundings in which a child lives and grows form the atmosphere which he breathes in at every moment and if there is poison in it, he inhales and imbibes the poison which becomes part of his substance and nature. A pure environment is needed for a pure life impulse to shape and develop itself.

*

What is the very central character of the child consciousness? It is confidence in life, the surety that nothing can baulk the fulfilment of life's purpose, the trust that overrides all set-backs and stumbles, gaily passes through dangers and difficulties. This confidence, this assurance the very body shares in and impels it to movements of daring and adventure. It is this that is the cause of the body's growth, and so long as it is maintained, keeps the body young. So the poet says:

> A simple child
> That lightly draws its breath,
> And feels its life in every limb,
> What should it know of death?[1]

Age sets in precisely when there is a fall in this self-confidence and assurance of the body consciousness, when the body begins to fear, becomes too cautious and apprehensive. A wound, a cut, even a broken limb would not stop a child normally to go forward with the same dash and carelessness. And that character is the source not only of his physical fitness and growth, but also that of a mental alacrity and soundness which is an inestimable possession of the child consciousness.

The wisest teacher is he who does not teach too much the wisdom of prudence and moderation, but encourages this *élan vital*, the life urge, in the child and yet seeks to organise and canalise it, as an efficient instrument of high ideals and purposes.

*

[1] Wordsworth: "We Are Seven".

24

There are two failing which a teacher must guard against – to which he is usually prone – if he wishes to secure respect and obedience and trust from children:

(1) telling a lie and
(2) losing temper.

A child can easily find out whether you are spinning a long yarn or not. He is inquisitive, irrepressively curious and, above all, he has his own manner and angle of looking at things. He puts questions about all things and subjects and in all ways that seem queer to an adult view. His answers too to questions, his solutions of problems are very unorthodox, bizarre. But it is all the more the task of the elder not only to put up with all these vagaries, but also with great sympathy and patience to appreciate and understand what the child attempts to express.

If you get irritated or angry and try to snub or brush him away, it would mean the end of all cordial relation between you and him. Or, again, if you try to hoodwink him, give a false answer to hide your ignorance, in that case too the child will not be deceived, he will find you out and lose all respect for you. It is far better to own your ignorance, saying you do not know than to pose as a knowing man; although that may affect to some extent his sense of hero-worship and he may not entertain any longer the unspoilt awe and esteem with which he was accustomed to look up to you, still you will not lose his affection and confidence.

Infinite patience and a temper that is never frayed or ruffled are demanded of the teacher and the parent who wish to guide and control successfully and happily a child.

With that you can mould in the end the most refractory child, without that you will fail even with a child of goodwill.

The Growing Child

PAVITRA

Modern education, on the whole, takes the child as an undeveloped body endowed with a young life, untrained sensibilities, acute but often unrestrained emotions, an immature mind and, as he grows, a nascent and groping reason. Reason is the highest recognized faculty, and to make of the fullgrown child a being goverened by reason and capable of discrimination and rational thinking with a healthy and strong body, a sensitive but chastened emotional and aesthetic being, well trained in the conventional morality and customs of the present day social life, will appear to many educationists an ideal achievement so far as the individual child is concerned. But society has its word to say; it requires a regular supply of young men and women, immediately serviceable for its complicated economic, administrative and industrial machinery and therefore demands that they should be classified according to ability and capacity. In the process of training, the child is submitted to the powerful (for his delicate and impressionable nature) influence of parents, teachers and schoolmates. Moreover the requirements of society to some extent run counter to the innate urge of the child. Thus the best of which the child would have been capable does not realize itself fully – far from it.

The defects of modern education are well known. They have often been described and analyzed. But the remedies that have been proposed are mere palliatives. They

27

counter the effects and not the cause. If we want to find a genuine solution to the present difficulties, we have to discover the cause of the evil and for that to re-examine the whole foundation on which education rests.

As early as 1910 when he was a political leader in Bengal, Sri Aurobindo propounded certain principles of education. At that time they were truly revolutionary as they broke away deliberately from the conventional notions on education that were then prevalent under the foreign domination. These principles, of which I quote here below the first one, most important and sufficient for my present purpose, did not seem to have attracted the attention they deserve and they remain even today practically unknown to the educational world.

"The first principle of true teaching is that nothing can be taught. The teacher is not an instructor or task-master, he is a helper and a guide. His business is to suggest and not to impose. He does not actually train the pupil's mind, he only shows him how to perfect his instruments of knowledge and helps and encourages him in the process. He does not impart knowledge to him, he shows him how to acquire knowledge for himself. He does not call forth the knowledge that is within; he only shows him where it lies and how it can be habituated to rise to the surface. The distinction that reserves this principle for the teaching of adolescent and adult minds and denies its application to the child, is a conservative and unintelligent doctrine. Child or man, boy or girl, there is only one sound principle of good teaching. Difference of age only serves to diminish or increase the amount of help and guidance necessary; it does not change its nature".[1]

[1] Sri Aurobindo. "A System of National Education", first published

Since the beginning of the century the educationists have been devoting themselves, especially in the West, to initiating and carrying out a considerable amount of theoretical and experimental research work in the field of education and child psychology and have come to conclusions similar to those expressed so forcefully by Sri Aurobindo. For them the child is foremost a developing being who has its own needs, different from an adult's and for that reason easily misunderstood by the adult. The first task of the educator is to make sure that the child's needs are satisfied and that the child is happy.

"New education...is really a new attitude towards the child. An attitude of understanding and love, and above all an attitude of respect. An attitude of expectation, of patience; the restraint of a delicate hand that dare not open a flower-bud nor disturb a baby in the midst of his first experiments, a student in the course of his early work...

"The child has within himself everything that is necessary for a true education, and particularly a ceaseless activity, incessantly revived, in which he is totally engrossed, the activity of a growing being who is continuously developing and to whom, for that very reason, our help may be useful, but our direction is not necessary."[2]

Speaking of this new trend in Western education, Sri Aurobindo regards it as a healthy step. It shows the

in the *Karmayogin* in 1910; reprinted in book form in 1921 and included in *Sri Aurobindo and the Mother on Education*, Sri Aurobindo International Centre of Education, Pondicherry, 3rd ed., 1966, p. 20.

[2] Roger Cousinet, *L'Education nouvelle*, Delachaux et Niestle, Neuchatel & Paris, 1950, pp. 20-21.

beginning of "... the realisation that each human being is a self-developing soul and that the business of both parent and teacher is to enable and to help the child to educate himself, to develop his own intellectual, moral, aesthetic and practical capacities and to grow freely as an organic being, not to be kneaded and pressured into form like an inert plastic material. It is not yet realised what this soul is or that the true secret, whether with child or man, is to help him to find his deeper self, the real psychic entity within. That, if we ever give it a chance to come forward, and still more if we call it into the foreground as 'the leader of the march set in our front,' will itself take up most of the business of education out of our hands and develop the capacity of the psychological being towards a realisation of its potentialities of which our present mechanical view of life and man and external routine methods of dealing with them prevent us from having any experience or forming any conception. These new educational methods are on the straight way to this truer dealing. The closer touch attempted with the psychical entity behind the vital and physical mentality and an increasing reliance on its possibilities must lead to the ultimate discovery that man is inwardly a soul and a conscious power of the Divine and that the evocation of this real man within is the right object of education and indeed of all human life if it would find and live according to the hidden Truth and deepest law of its own being."[1]

How this is to be brought about is mainly a matter of tactful dealing with the child. Of course, there must be a great freedom in the choice of the subjects, in the time

[1] Sri Aurobindo, *The Human Cycle*, Ch. III.

30

allotted to each subject, so that the child can progress at his own pace. This last result calls for individual handling and a sufficient knowledge of the language by the child so as to be able to read and comprehend. Textbooks are usually too condensed, therefore work on files or work-sheets is preferable, but their preparation imposes a heavy burden on the teacher. Anyhow a real FREE PRO-GRESS CLASS – as these classes may be called – can only begin when the child is able to read and write fairly well, i.e., in Class IV or V.

Before that level, the teacher has to use his own discretion. But the right attitude towards the child must be adopted from the very beginning, in the Kidnergarten. A child's soul is usually very close to the surface and, if a proper environment is maintained, it will continue to be so for several years.

Ordinary education and the influence of adult society usually act to muffle and distort this happy and healthy spontaneity, and replace it by an automatism based on the more or less arbitrary conventions of family and society and no less arbitrary rules of moral or religious education.

In order to awaken the child to the understanding of the relations existing between the two worlds which he discovers almost simultaneously – the inner and the outer – he should be told how to observe carefully what happens in himself. He has to be shown that he is the playground, sometimes the battlefield of different forces and inner movements: sensations, impulses, emotions, ideas. And he must be taught how to distinguish between them practically and find out their nature and origin. For this discovery intellectual explanations are insufficient, it is no use lecturing and moralizing. It is with concrete instances,

31

from the day to day school life, taking advantage of apparently insignificant incidents, that the discrimination can be slowly developed.

The child will then be shown that it is possible to rise above the fleeting inner movements that he has now learnt to discriminate and not to be frightened by the inner silence in which he may enter – this silence that will later reveal itself as a plenitude.

As an illustration, I shall give the case when a tense situation has somehow arisen and a decision has to be taken, or when an obstacle hampers all progress. At a suitable time, the teacher may call the child when alone, present to him impartially, in a few kind and simple words, the consequences of the possible alternatives, then ask him to consider quietly the whole matter and, after a moment of silence, to aspire for light and truth. Not by the mind and the reason, because truth does not depend on arguments, nor by the emotions, although restrained and purified emotions will greatly contribute to reaching a solution by their quietness, but in the freedom, impartiality and equality of the spirit, the teacher may succeed in imparting the little touch which, by its repetition, will awaken the still receptive young being to the presence of the inner divinity. What the child then decides must not be questioned, he should be allowed to proceed; he knows the consequences and will remember them. Thus only will the child acquire the sense of responsibility which is aimed at.

The justification of this attitude is given by Sri Aurobindo in these terms: "All experience shows that man must be given a certain freedom to stumble in action as well as to err in knowledge so long as he does not get from within himself his freedom from wrong movement and error; otherwise he cannot grow."[1]

Thus the child will be shown by experience that there is in him, above the movements of the ordinary nature – likes and dislikes, impulses and fancies, ideas, etc., – a region of deep peace and silence. If he listens carefully he will discover that in this silence, there is also the feeling of a Presence, a conscious Presence. And after some time, when he turns back to his problems, he will be found one day to say: "Oh! I know now what to do!" The quality of such decisions is very different from the ordinary movements. The child will recognize gradually that this inner guidance is the only valid and most satisfying one, it alone gives a peace and joy that surpass pleasures and enjoyments, but it is difficult to discover and listen to, because emotions and thoughts are too active and noisy – an inner silence has to be established first. If the teacher succeeds in establishing with his pupil a soul to soul contact, a kind of helpful link is created.

The Mother has shown how a proper relation between teacher and pupil can be established and maintained.

"When a child has made a mistake, see that he confesses it to you spontaneously and frankly; and when he has confessed, make him understand with kindness and affection what was wrong in his movement and that he should not repeat it. In any case, never scold him; a fault confessed must be forgiven. You should not allow any fear to slip in between you and your child; fear is a disastrous way to education: invariably it gives birth to dissimulation and falsehood. An affection that sees clear, that is firm yet

[1] Sri Aurobindo, *The Human Cycle*, Ch. XXI.

gentle and a sufficiently practical knowledge will create bonds of trust that are indispensable for you to make the education of your child effective."[1]

Threat and punishment should be completely avoided. An untimely outburst from the teacher is all that is needed to wipe out all the confidence that the child has in him; the way will be blocked for a long time and often irreparably. Love and sympathy, desire to help, devotion to an ideal, the satisfaction of being at peace with oneself, are in the end more potent constructive forces than fear of punishment, whether by the headmaser, the police or a god. "...coercion," says Sri Aurobindo, "only chains up the devil and alters at best his form of action into more mitigated and civilised movements; it does not and cannot eliminate him."[2]

But this should not lead one to believe that we advocate a freedom which allows the child to indulge indiscriminately his desires and caprices. The freedom we vindicate for the child is the freedom to establish the conditions of his own progress – hence the name FREE PROGRESS CLASSES, as we like to call the classes of our method. Being, so to say, his own master, the child is obliged to refer constantly to the inner guidance, if he wants to avoid pitfalls, because experience will have taught him the price he has to pay in the shape of loss of inner harmony and peace, clouding of the mind and dissipation of his time and energy. This necessity of perpetual choice is the creative element in this education; its aim is to inculcate in

[1] *The Mother on Education*, reprinted in *Sri Aurobindo and the Mother on Education*, 3rd. ed., 1966, p. 56.

[2] Sri Aurobindo, *The Human Cycle*, Ch. XXI.

the student a spirit of self-reliance and responsibility. Nothing can be a better gift to a growing child. And we allow him the freedom to err or stumble, because we know that by his errors and stumblings he will be able to walk straight.

35

Children: Right Educators

M. P. PANDIT

[This paper is based on the letters of Sri Aurobindo in which two questions were put to the Master. They are most meaningful for parents and teachers alike.]

I

What is the way to make children imbibe yogic qualities like equality, aptitude for harmony, etc.?

The one unfailing way is to cultivate and naturalise these qualities in oneself first before seeking to educate others in the direction. Nothing impresses the child-mind so much as example; precept without practice fails to carry much conviction. If the teacher carries these qualities as part of his nature, then there is an effortless radiation of their power among the students who come under his influence. No doubt the effect is not the same on all. Natures that are raw may not respond at all, some may come to admire mentally and do nothing more. But there would be at least a few who would seek to emulate and grow in these qualities.

Children need constant encouragement by way of approval, praise, etc. But they do not like to be shown their mistakes; they get sullen. What is the way out?

It is not merely the young that resent being shown their mistakes; even the older ones do not like it. However, it is something in the human nature which resists change.

The ideal way is to make the child itself see its mistakes. The teacher should so arrange things that the same error is repeated again and again forcing the child to ask why it happens that way. It is at that moment when the mind is ready that the teacher should lend a helping hand and point out what is to be remedied. Lessons learnt in this way do not hurt the dignity of the child and form part of its knowledge for all time.

II

I am a teacher trying to build the minds of the youngsters in my charge in the mould of the great. For this purpose I find Sri Aurobindo's literature very helpful by reason of its integrating approach and object. Could you suggest the order in which their books could best be studied or read? Will this reading help in the formation of their character?

Naturally writings of great people breathe the greatness of the authors. Especially when the authors are spiritual personalities of the stamp of Sri Aurobindo and the Mother, their words are alive with the spiritual power characteristic of their manifestation. In a concrete sense they – in this case, Sri Aurobindo and the Mother – are present in each line, each word of their utterance. Such powerful writings cannot but exert a deep influence on impressionable minds though the results may not be always immediately perceptible.

37

It has always seemed to me that it is the teachers who need to be taught to study more than the students. They have to imbibe thoroughly the spirit of the Wisdom they are to communicate before they are in a position to teach effectively. Sri Aurobindo and the Mother have written pointedly on the aim of education, the conditions under which it can be best carried out, the requirements of a successful teacher, and the several methods which are to be adopted to suit the varying types of children. Their entire conception of education is something revolutionary: the teacher and the student often exchange their roles; the teacher becomes conscious of the sacred character of his mission as he learns his true function. Each teacher should read and reread the book *On Education* by Sri Aurobindo and the Mother.

What books to be chosen for the students depends upon their mental growth and background. Selections from the earlier poems of Sri Aurobindo, the *Baji Prabhou*, selections from his translations of Ramayana and Mahabharata, the book The Mother, *Tales of All Time*, edited by the Mother, selections from *Words of Long Ago, Words of the Mother* may be drawn upon.

Foundation of the Whole

FRIEDRICH FROEBEL

The development and formation of the whole future life of each being is contained in the beginning of its existence. The untroubled realisation and the undiminished efficiency of the life of each being depend wholly on the comprehension and fostering, on the recognition and firm carrying out of this beginning.

Man, as a child, resembles the flower on the plant, the blossom on the tree; as these are in relation to the tree, so is the child in relation to humanity – a young bud, a fresh blossom; and as such, it bears, includes, and proclaims the ceaseless reappearance of new human life.

As the flower bud of the tree – connected with twig, branch, and trunk, with the whole ramification of root and crown, and, through this double ramification, with earth and heaven – stands in united coherence and reciprocal exchange with the whole universe for the development and vivification of its being, so stands man also, in all-sided developing life-exchange with nature, with humanity, and with all spiritual efforts and influences – with the universal life.

The blissful development of the human being which leads to perfection and completion, and the fitting him for the attainment of his destiny, and thus for the attainment by effort of the genuine joy and true peace of life, depend alone on the correct comprehension of man, even as a child, in respect to his nature as well as to his relations, and on the corresponding treatment of man in accordance with this nature and these relations.

But man is a created being, and, as such, is at the same time a part and a whole (therefore, a part-whole), for, on the one side, he is, as a creation, a part of the universe; but, on the other side, he is also a whole, since – just because he is a creature – the nature of his Creator (a living and creating nature full of life, and testifying to life, therefore in itself single) lives in him.

This original and fundamental nature of man, as being life in itself and therefore again giving life, makes itself known in man's impulse to creative formation. This fundamental nature makes itself known even in the child by the instinct for observing, analyzing, and again uniting – that is, by the instinct for formative and creative activity. Indeed, the fostering of this instinct in the child makes manifest the life of man, at the same time wholly satisfying the demands of that life.

Man, as a child, appears to be conditioned and mediated by father and mother.

Father, mother and child form a triune life-whole – a family. The child creates the family and the family-life by its advent; and, on the other hand, man's continuous presence on earth is indispensably linked with the family. The family and child reciprocally condition each other; neither exists without the other; they form in themselves an inseparable unit.

As in his original advent in the universe (on the earth), so also in the family man again makes his appearance as a true part-whole, since he is a whole in himself, and also, at the same time, a necessary member of the family life-whole.

Only as a member of the family will it be possible for man to become a symmetrical, real, whole man; indeed, the family as a whole is a real, whole, human existence, and the family life as a whole is real, complete, human life.

As now the family is the fundamental condition of the production of man and the mediator of his existence, so also man as a child attains fully the development of his instinct for creative self-activity only when connected with and conditioned by the family; then only is it possible for him to live in complete accordance with this instinct.

All genuine human education and true human training, and so also this endeavour of ours, are linked with the quiet fostering in the family of this instinct for activity, with the thoughtful development of the child for the satisfaction of this instinct, and with the fitting of the child to be active in conformity with it.

It is the aim of our endeavour to make it possible for man freely and spontaneously to develop, to educate himself from his first advent on earth, as a whole human being, as a whole in himself, and in harmony and union with the life-whole – to make it possible for him to inform and instruct himself, to recognize himself thus as a definite member of the all-life, and, as such, freely and spontaneously to make himself known – freely and spontaneously to live.

Moreover, the first and fundamental appearance of love – of the love of parents and child, the family-love – is found now in the family-life; indeed, the family is love itself become personal. The parental love manifests itself in its whole nature just in and by means of the nourishing and developing of the child's impulse to creative activity, and in the supplying of the means for this development. The fostering of this impulse arouses and strengthens the love of brothers and sisters. This fostering of the impulse to creative activity is thus a comprehensive expression of the true love of parents and child, of the genuine family-love, and so reveals, and at the same time wholly satisfies, all love and the nature of love.

Considering man as a created being, it is also quite indispensable to regard and treat him, even in childhood as well as through his whole life, as a creative being, and to train and prepare him so that, while himself creating, he may, even from his earliest years, find and recognize the Creator, the creation, and the created, and may thus find and recognize himself in this threefold relation and connection according to the measure of his increasing capacity.

So trained, he will be enabled to understand and comprehend, and thus to attain to that which is man's calling and destiny as an earthly being – namely, to recognize God in the creation and in the creature, and therefore in man; to recognize himself in himself and in mankind; and thus each in the others, and the others in each individual: to promote this recognition, to represent it and to make it representable, to perceive it and to make it perceptible.

But to see, to recognize, and to perceive, require and presuppose light and almost are light. Recognition therefore develops light in and around the human being, from the satisfying fostering of his impulse to creative and observant activity. The destiny and calling of man (to be light and to move in light), as well as the possibility for him by the fostering of the impulse to creative activity to fulfil the above-mentioned destiny, is thus shown to us.

As we now see man, even from his first appearance upon the earth and his first entrance into the family, move in a threefold way, which is yet single in itself (therefore a triune way), in and by means of life, in and by means of love, in light and by means of light – in his seeing, perceiving, recognizing, and remembering – we also see that the careful fostering of his impulse to creative activity completely corresponds to and satisfies this triune life of man. But this triune way in which man moves is, above all comparison, important to the human being; for God shows himself in Nature, in the universe, as life; God reveals himself in humanity as love (and in love); and God manifests himself in wisdom (in the spirit) as light and in light. So God is the life, the love, and the light; and in such a triune way he appears as the Creator and in the creature.

In life, love, and light, and as life, love, and light therefore, the being and nature of the child, of the man, are made known as existing, are revealed as having been realized and as still realizing.

By life, the child appears predominantly connected with Nature, with the all; by love, he appears pre-eminently united with humanity; and by light, he appears to be one with wisdom, with God.

Man as a created being is thus in his first period of life on earth to be regarded, considered, and fostered in the all-sidedness of his relations as a threefold child, as it were; or, as a child in three separate relations which are united in themselves – as a child of Nature, as a human child, and as a child of God; that is, first, according to his common, earthly, and natural conditions and connections, according to his life; then, according to his special human existence, to his love; finally, according to his original spiritual nature, his anticipations and perceptions, his remembrance, recognitions, and intentions, his knowledge and his wisdom.

In his first relation (as a child of Nature) man is to be considered as a being bound, chained, unconscious, subject to impulses, sentient, living only corporeally; in the latter relation, as a child of God, as a free being not only fitted for consciousness, destined to consciousness, but already in anticipation conscious of his nature, therefore following by his own will a high and genuine unity of life as a thoughtful, perceptive, intuitive, spiritual, knowing, and wise being; and in the intermediate relation (as a child of humanity) as a being struggling from bondage and chains towards freedom; from singleness toward unity, toward consciousness; from separation toward union, toward peace; an aspiring being devoted constantly to the above-named efforts; and, in the anticipation of finding unity, a joyously living being.

To become clearly conscious of all the conditions and relations in which and by means of which man exists, and to faithfully live up to the requirements of these conditions and relations, make man (as a presence) first become man in consciousness and action; and make it possible for him to become a whole, complete human being by leading him to an equally careful and joyous fulfilment of each of his duties, and by making it possible for him to fulfil the totality of the duties of man in harmony.

Only if the child, the human being, be comprehended and treated through the whole fostering of the impulse of his life (his impulse to creative activity), in the triunity of his nature, as living, loving, and perceiving, in the unity of his life, in the all-sidedness of his circumstances and relations; if he be comprehended and treated as an earthly being in accordance with what he is, what he has, and what he will become; only if he comprehends the outer world around him in like triunity (and thus recognizes the revelation of the divine in like triunity) in its unity, in each individual, and in the sum of all unities – only thus can man develop himself as that which he is, as the manifold and articulated (but in himself single) whole, and, at the same time, a member of the great whole – of all life; only thus can he develop himself in conformity with his destiny, and be faithful to his vocation.

He will thus form an entirety and a unity of life from and around himself, and, in and by means of his creative life, God, Nature, and humanity will reveal themselves in unity and singleness. Man himself will make them known as they reveal themselves to him in and for the all-sided union, the genuine peace, and the true joy of life.

Goal-Forming Activity of the Child

ALFRED ADLER

The fundamental fact in human development is the dynamic and purposive striving of the psyche. A child, from its earliest infancy, is engaged in a constant struggle to develop, and this struggle is in accordance with an unconsciously formed but ever-presnt goal – a vision of greatness, perfection and superiority. This struggle, this goal-forming activity, reflects, of course, the peculiarly human faculty of thinking and of imagining, and it dominates all our specific acts throughout life. It dominates even our thoughts, for we do not think objectively but in accordance with the goal and style of life we have formed.

The unity of personality is implicit in each human being's existence. Every individual represents both a unity of personality and the individual fashioning of that unity. The individual is thus both the picture and the artist. He is the artist of his own personality, but as an artist he is neither an infallible worker, nor a person with a complete understanding of soul and body – he is rather a weak, extremely fallible and imperfect human being.

In considering the construction of a personality, the chief defect to be noted is that its unity, its particular style and goal, is not built upon objective reality, but upon the subjective view the individual takes of the facts of life. A conception, a view of a fact, is never the fact itself, and it is for this reason that human beings, all of whom live in the same world of facts, mould themselves differently.

Each one organises himself according to his personal view of things, and some views are more sound, and some views are less sound. We must always reckon with these individual mistakes and failures in the development of a human being. Especially must we reckon with the misinterpretations made in early childhood, for these dominate the subsequent course of our existence.

A concrete instance of this may be seen in this clinical case. A woman, at the age of fifty-two, was always disparaging women who were older than herself. She related the fact that when she was a tiny child, she always felt humiliated and undervalued because of an older sister, who received all the attention.

Looking at this case with what we might call the "vertical" point of view of Individual Psychology, we can see the same mechanism, the same psychological dynamics both at the beginning of her life and at present – that is to say, near the close of her existence. There is always the fear of being undervalued and the anger and irritation at finding others favoured or preferred. Even if we knew nothing else of this woman's life, or of her particular unity of personality, we could almost fill in the gaps in our knowledge on the basis of the two facts given.

The psychologist acts here like a novelist, who has to construct a human being with a definite line of action, style of life, or pattern of behaviour, and has to construct him in such a way that the impression of a unified personality is not disturbed. A good psychologist would be able to predict the conduct of this woman in certain situations, and to describe clearly the traits which accompany this particular "life line" in her personality.

The striving or goal-forming activity, which is responsible for the construction of individual personalities, presupposes another important psychological fact. This is the sense or feeling of inferiority which stimulates the imagination and incites attempts to dissipate the psychological sense of inferiority by bettering the situation. A bettering of one's situation results in a lessening of the feeling of inferiority. From a psychological point of view it may be regarded as a compensation.

Now the important thing about the sense of inferiority and the mechanism of psychological compensation is that it opens up a vast possibility of making mistakes. The sense of inferiority may stimulate objective accomplishment; it may also result in a purely psychological adjustment which widens the gulf between the individual and objective reality. Or, again, the sense of inferiority may appear so tragic that the only way it can be overcome is by the development of psychological compensatory traits, which in the end may not overcome the situation at all but which are nonetheless psychologically necessary and inevitable.

There are, for example, three classes of children who manifest very clearly the development of compensatory traits. They are children who come into the world with weak or imperfect organs; children who are treated with severity and with no affection; and, finally, children who receive too much pampering.

We may take these three classes of children as exemplifying three basic situations in terms of which the development of the more normal types of children may be studied and understood. Not every child is born a cripple, but it is surprising how many children manifest, to a greater or lesser degree, psychological traits based on some physical difficulty or weak organ – psychological traits of which the archetype may be studied in the extreme case of the crippled child.

And as for the classifications of pampered and hated children, practically all children fall to a greater or lesser degree into one, or even both groupings.

All these three primary situations produce a feeling of insufficiency and inferiority, and by way of reaction, an ambition beyond the realm of human possibility. The sense of inferiority and the striving for superiority are always two phases of the same fundamental fact in human life, and are thus inseparable. In pathological situations, it is difficult to say whether it is the exaggerated feeling of inferiority, or the exacerbated striving for superiority which is most harmful. They both go together in more or less rhythmical waves.

In the case of children we find the inordinate ambition, aroused by an exaggerated sense of inferiority, acting like a poison in the soul – forever making the child dissatisfied. Such a dissatisfaction is not one which leads to useful activity. It remains fruitless because it is fed by a disproportionate ambition. This ambition may be seen twisting itself into character traits and personal mannerisms. It acts like a perpetual irritant making the individual supersensitive and on guard lest he be hurt or trodden upon.

Types of this nature – and the annals of Individual Psychology are full of them – develop into persons whose abilities remain dormant, persons who become, as we say, "nervous", or eccentric. Persons of these types, when driven too far, wind up in the world of the irresponsible and the criminal because they think only of themselves and not of others. Their egotism, both moral and psychological, becomes absolute.

We find some of them avoiding reality and objective facts and constructing a new world for themselves. By day-dreaming, by hugging imaginative fantasies as if they represented reality, they finally succeed in creating psychological peace. They have reconciled reality and the mind by constructing reality in the image of the mind.

In all such developments the tel-tale criterion which needs to be watched by the psychologist and by the parent is the degree of social feeling which the child or individual manifests. Social feeling is the crucial and deciding factor in normal development. Every disturbance which results in a lessening of the social or communal feeling has a tremendously harmful effect on the mental growth of the child. Social feeling is the barometer of the child's normality.

It is around the principle of social feeling that Individual Psychology has developed its pedagogical technique. Parents or guardians must not permit a child to attach himself to one person only. If this is permitted the child will find himself badly or insufficiently prepared for later life.

A good way of finding out the degree of social feeling of a child is to observe him at the time when he enters school. On entering school the child meets with one of his earliest and severest tests. The school is a new situation for the child: it will therefore reveal how well the child has been prepared to face new situations, and particularly how well he has been prepared to meet new persons.

It is the general lack of knowledge as to how to prepare a child for school that explains why so many adults look back on their school years as a sort of nightmare. Of course the school, when properly administered, will often make up for the deficiencies in the earlier rearing of the children. The ideal school should serve as a mediator between the home and the wide world of reality, and should be a place not merely for book knowledge, but a place in which the knowledge and art of living should be taught. But while we are waiting for the ideal school to develop so that it may overcome the deficiencies in the parental education of children, we can also put our finger on the faults of the parents.

For analyzing the faults of family upbringing the school may serve as an indicator, precisely because it is not yet an ideal environment. Children who have not been taught how to make contact with others feel themselves alone when they enter school. As a result they are regarded as peculiar, and thus the initial tendency grows stronger and stronger with time. Their proper development is thwarted, and they become behaviour problem children. People blame the school in such cases, although the school has here merely brought out the latent defects in the home education.

It has always been an open question to Individual Psychology whether behaviour problem children can make any progress in school at all. We have always been able to prove that it is a danger sign when a child begins to fail at school. It is a sign not so much of failure in studies but of psychological failure. It means that the child has begun to lose faith in himself. Discouragement has made its appearance, and the child begins to avoid useful roads and normal tasks, searching all the time for another outlet, a road to freedom and easy success. Instead of the

51

road which society has mapped out, he chooses a private road where he can erect a compensation for his inferiority by attaining a sense of superiority. He chooses the path that is always attractive to discouraged individuals – the path of quickest psychological success.

It is easier to distinguish one's self and to give one's self the feeling of a conqueror by throwing off social and moral responsibilities and by breaking the law, than by following the established social paths. But this easy road to superiority is always an indication of underlying cowardice and weakness, no matter what apparent daring and bravery are manifested in the outward acts. Such a person always tries to do those things in which he is certain to succeed, thus showing off his superiority.

Just as we observe that criminals, despite their apparent recklessness and bravery, are at bottom cowardly, so we have been able to see how children in less dangerous situations betray their sense of weakness by various small signs. Thus we commonly see children (and for that matter adults, too) who are not able to stand upright but must always lean against something.

Under the old methods of training children and the old ways of understanding such signs, the symptom was treated but not the underlying situation. One used to say to such a child. "Don't lean on something all the time." Actually what matters here is not that the child leans, but that he always feels the need of a support. One can readily persuade the child, either by punishment or reward, to give up this sign of weakness, but his great need for support is not thereby relieved. The disease continues. It is a good educator who can read signs and can eradicate the underlying disease with sympathy and understanding.

52

From a single sign one can often draw conclusions as to the presence of many qualities or traits. In the case of a child obsessed with the need of leaning on something, we can see at once that such traits as anxiety and dependence are sure to be present. By comparing him with similar persons whose case we know thoroughly, we can reconstruct such a personality, and we can see, in short, that we have to deal with a pampered child.

We turn now to the character traits of another class of children – those who have gone without love. The traits of this class, in their most developed form, can be observed by studying the biographies of all the great enemies of humanity. In all the life stories of these men the one thing that stands out is the fact that as children they were badly treated. In this way they developed a hardness of character, envy and hatred. They could not bear to see others happy.

Now, envious persons of this type are found not merely among straight villains but among supposedly normal persons. Such individuals when they have charge of children think that the children should not be any happier than they themselves were as children. We find such a view applied by parents to their children, as well as by guardians to the children of others who are put in their charge.

Such a view, such thoughts, do not spring from bad intentions. They simply reflect the mentality of those who have bern harshly brought up. Such persons can produce any number of good reasons and maxims, as for example, "Spare the rod and spoil the child!" And they give us endless proofs and examples, which do not quite convince us inasmuch as the futility of a rigid, authoritative education is proved by the simple fact that it estranges the child from his educator.

By exploring various symptoms and interrelating them, the psychologist can, after some practice, organise a system by the aid of which the hidden psychological processes of an individual may be revealed. While every point which we examine by this system reflects something of the complete personality of the individual under investigation, we can feel satisfied only when we get the same indications at every point of our examination. Individual Psychology is thus an art as well as a science, and it cannot be too much emphasised that the speculative scheme, the system of concepts, is not to be applied in a wooden and mechanical fashion to an individual under examination.

In all investigations the primary thing is to study the individual; we must never draw far-reaching conclusions from one or two modes of expression, but we must look for all possible supporting phases. Only when we are successful in confirming our tentative hypothesis, only when we have been able, for example, to find the same stubbornness or discouragement permeates the entire personality.

In this connection it must be remembered that the subject under examination has no understanding of his own forms of expression and is thus unable to conceal his true self. We see his personality in action, and his personality is revealed not by what he says or thinks about himself but by his acts interpreted in their context. It is not that the patient deliberately wants to lie to us, but we have learned to recognize a vast gulf between a man's conscious thoughts and his unconscious motivations – a gulf which

54

can best be bridged by a disinterested but sympathetic outsider. The outsider – whether he be the psychologist, or the parent or the teacher – should learn to interpret a personality on the basis of objective facts seen as the expression of the purposive, but more or less unconscious, strivings of the individual.

Thus the attitude of the individual with regard to the three fundamental questions of individual and social life reveals his true self as nothing else can.

(1) The first of these questions is the social relation, which we have already discussed in the context of the contrast between the private and objective views of reality. But the social relation manifests itself also as a specific task – it is the task of making friends and getting along with people. How does the individual meet that problem? What is his answer? When a human being believes he can evade the question by saying that the matter of friends, the matter of social relationships is of complete indifference to him, then indifference is his answer. From this indifference we can, of course, draw conclusions as to the direction and organization of his personality.

It is to be noted, moreover, that the social relation is not confined merely to the physical making of friends and meeting of people; all the abstract qualities like friendship, comradeship, truthfulness and loyalty cluster about this relation, and the answer to the social relation indicates the individual's answer on all these points.

(2) The second great question concerns how the individual wants to make use of his life – what part he wants to take in the general division of labour. If the social question may be said to be determined by the existence of

more than one ego, by the relationship I-you, then we may say that this question is determined by the fundamental relationship Man-Earth.

If one could reduce all mankind into one person, this person would have mutuality with the earth. What does he want from the earth? Just as in the case of the first question, the solution of the problem of occupation is not a one-sided or private matter, but a matter between man and earth. It is a two-sided relationship in which man hasn't got it all his own way. Success is determined not by our private will but in relation to objective realities. For this reason the answer that an individual makes, and the manner in which he makes it, to the question of occupation throws a very revealing light on his personality and on his attitude towards life.

(3) The third fundamental question arises from the fact that mankind is divided into two sexes. The solution of this problem is again not a private, subjective matter, but must be solved according to the inherent objective logic of the relationship. What is my position towards the other sex? The typical private conception is again a mistaken conception. A correct solution can be arrived at only through a careful consideration of all the questions which cluster around the sex relationship. And it stands to reason that every departure from a correct solution of the problem of love and marriage indicates a mistake, an error in the personality. Also many of the harmful consequences that follow a wrong solution of this problem are to be interpreted in the light of the underlying error of personality.

We can see, therefore, that we are in a position to discover the general style of life and particular goal of an individual from the way in which he answers these three questions. The goal is omnipotent. It decides a person's style of life and it will be reflected in every one of his acts. Thus if the goal is a striving towards being a fellow man, a goal directed to the useful side of life, the stamp of that goal will be apparent in the individual's solutions of all his problems. All the solutions will reflect constructive usefulness and the individual will have the sense of happiness and the feeling of worth and power that go with constructive and useful activity. If the goal is directed otherwise, if it is directed to the private and useless side of life, the individual will find himself unable to solve fundamental problems, and he will also lack the joy that comes from their proper solution.

There is a strong interconnection between all these fundamental problems, and it is made all the stronger by the fact that in the course of social life specific tasks spring out of these fundamental problems which can be carried out properly only in a social or communal setting, or, in other words, on the basis of social feeling. These tasks begin in the earlist years of childhood, when our sense-organs are developing in accordance with the stimulus of social life, in looking, speaking, hearing – in our relations to our brothers, sisters, parents, relatives, acquaintances, comrades, friends and teachers. They continue through life in the same manner, so that he who gets out of social touch with his fellows is lost.

The Adult and the Child

MARIA MONTESSORI

The amazingly rapid progress in the care and education of children in recent years may be attributed partly to a generally higher standard of life, but still more to an awakening of conscience. Not only is there an increasing concern for child health – it began in the last decade of the XIXth century – but also a new awareness of the personality of the child as something of the highest importance. Today it is impossible to go deeply into any branch of medicine or philosophy or sociology without taking account of the contribution brought by a knowledge of child life. A parallel, but on a lesser scale, is the light thrown by embryology on physiology in general and on evolution. But the study of the child, not in his physical but in his psychological aspect, may have an infinitely wider influence, extending to all human questions. In the mind of the child we may perhaps find the key to progress, and, who knows, the beginning of a new civilisation.

The Swedish poet and author, Ellen Key, prophesied that our century would be the century of the child. While anyone with patience to hunt through historical documents would find a recurrence of such ideas in the first King's Speech of King Victor Emmanuel III in Italy, when, in 1900, at the turn of the century, he succeeded to the throne after the assassination of his predecessor. He spoke of the new era beginning with the new century, and he too spoke of it as the Century of the Child.

It would seem that such almost prophetic glimpses arose from the impression produced by the investigations of science in the last ten years of the XIXth century; from the picture they gave of the child in sickness, ten times more exposed than the adult to death from infectious disease, or of the child as victim in harsh schools. No one could have foreseen then that the child held within himself a secret of life, able to lift the veil from the mysteries of the human soul; that he represented an unknown quantity, the discovery of which might enable the adult to solve his individual and social problems. This aspect may prove the foundation of a new science of child study, capable of influencing the whole social life of man...

The page of human history that tells the adventures of man as mind has yet to be read – of the child as through his senses he encounters obstacles and finds himself involved in insuperable conflicts with the grown-up who is stronger than he, who masters him without understanding him. Here was a blank page that had yet to receive the story of the unrealised sufferings that convulse the intact and delicate spiritual existence of the child, organising in his subconscious a lower man, different from what nature had intended....

Round the child therefore a new field of scientific exploration has come into being, distinct from psycho-analysis, its sole parallel. It implies essentially a form of assistance to the psychic life of infancy, and is concerned with normality and with education. Its characteristic is therefore the ascertainment of psychological facts as yet unknown to the child, and at the same time an awakening of the adult, who, in regard to the child, adopts mistaken attitudes that have their root in the subconscious....

Now if the child is to receive a different treatment from what it receives today, in order to save it from conflicts endangering its psychic life, there is a first, fundamental, essential step to be taken, on which all will depend – the modification of the adult. Indeed, if the adult is already doing all he can, and, as he will say, loves the child to the point of sacrifice, he acknowledges that he is faced by an insuperable problem. He must necessarily seek beyond what is known, voluntary and conscious.

Even in the child there is much that is unknown. There is a part of the soul of the child that has always been unknown, and that must be known. In the child, too, there is need for the discovery that will lead us to the unknown. For besides the child observed and studied by psychology and education, there remains the unknown child. We must seek for him in a spirit of enthusiasm, like those who know of hidden gold, and who explore unknown lands and move mountains in search of the precious metal. This is what the adult must do in searching for this unknown something hidden in the soul of the child. This is the labour in which all must partake, without distinction of caste, race or nation, for it will mean the bringing forth of an indispensable factor for the moral progress of humanity.

New Trends in Child Education

NORMAN C. DOWSETT

Today, students can reckon to spend ten to fifteen years of their early life in school. Three-fourths of their waking hours will be spent in the classroom. How important do we consider these years of the living growth in relation to learning and environment? These are the formative years of a person's life and as such it is quite probably that most of the important mental, vital and physical experiences of consciousness occur within the environment of school life.

It is well known among psychiatrists that it is easiest to recall those experiences of early life in the classroom. These experiences seem to impress themselves so powerfully on the child mind that they can often be vividly remembered at the end of life. Especially is this so, if the experiences are of a nature to upraise the ego or enhance the image of the personality. Old people delight in recalling how they came first in a certain subject, how much they loved a certain teacher, how a certain incident or experience changed the whole course of their lives. Rarely are the recollections of an unpleasant character unless, in the hands of the psychiatrist, the depths of the subconscious are explored and released from inhibitions and mental blocks, the tragedies of the past are unearthed and Pandora's Box is opened to reveal the complex horrors long buried in the unhappy forgetfulness of early childhood.

As educationists seeking perfection, it is incumbent

upon us to see that the human being of the future shall look back with a sense of gratitude and joy on his school life; where learning was first a play, a delight of activity leading to endless vistas of wonder, discovery and creativity; where time went swiftly on the wings of an immense enthusiasm, a love for life. Love for materials: pens, paper, paints and books. Love for people: friends, comrades, teachers and those who help. Love for learning and the opportunity to think. Love for the room, the desk, the reference books, the aids and apparatuses. Love for the all-inclusive joy of physical play and exercise, emotional expression of creativity and intellectual exploration into new realms of thought. Love for the sheer joy and privilege of just being a member of a school community. Surely, such love one would have continue even after school!

Fifty years ago sucn an ideal was hardly possible. Most students longed for the day when they could leave school; eager to be released from the irksome discipline and confusing atmosphere of the classroom for the unknown adventure and discovery of the great wide world which was less to be feared than the inevitable petty punishments and teacher dominations of the classroom. Today with more money being spent on education, there are multiple classrooms but many teachers are lacking in imagination on the best use to make of their rooms, for creating an atmosphere conducive to impressionable experience. The higher the class, the less important is considered the atmosphere of the room. Why? Because the teacher, the reader, the lecturer, the professor is more important – what he says must create the atmosphere – not what the student does or says or attempts. So long as we think in terms of a "teacher-dominated class" this will remain the state of affairs.

I would, however, suggest that even on the highest levels a classroom could become virtually a work-room, where all the "tools" of the student's needs are at hand. Where those who want to listen to a particular lecture can do so through the earphones of a tape recorder while the others pursue their various interests in the same subject in writing or reading, discussion groups or a tutorial project with the teacher. In this way, whenever a special or particular problem arises it would be possible to deal with it there and then, not at some future date or in some later period.

The room should attract the student to work, awaken his interest in the subject, challenge his sense of discovery in an atmosphere redolent with ideas. Ideally, it should be a fixed room, given over entirely to the needs of the subject and the progressive demands of the students. It should evolve with the students' own evolution. So will it grow in stature to the experience of each student and bear the imprint of his passing, creating a legend, a story, a tradition that was lived.

*

Whatever we consider is the object of education, we cannot ignore the fact that it has to be built on a firm foundation. That foundation has to take cognisance of the need to find some basis of identification, between what man *is* and what he *does*. In spite of Plato's declaration that "Man is a creature who at every moment of his existence must examine and scrutinize the conditions of his existence... a being in search of meaning" we still continue to cram informational knowledge into students and consider this sufficient to equip them for a life in today's world of cybernetic existentialism challenging a new form of symbiosis where mutually beneficial partnerships could bring about world unity.

The only basis for any education must surely start with the student himself, because all truth and meaning are within. Unless he uncovers the meaning of his existence, equates this with the purpose of his work in life, there will be no progress towards perfection, no evolution towards the manifestation of truth, no claim to the high dignity of man and the heritage of the human race. What then is the value of his existence, if he has worked and laboured never to have lived at all?

It is because man today has recognised the fact that he must know himself before he can know his world that he continues to learn, study, search for truth to the end of life. Is it not then imperative that he lay the foundation of his learning at school, when the mind is young, plastic, open to new ideas? A new morality has to take the place of the old. Not of prohibition but of a new creativity – a morality of inner experience which will be recognised as the true authority for all our scientific, artistic and philosophic activity. Education through yoga-sadhana can alone give this authority. Once a student's mind and character have been built on the basis of this authority with the strength and confidence it enjoys, what then will stop him from earning his own living?

*

One of the greatest problems presented to progressive and forward-looking teachers is the position of today's parent in relation to the growth-experiences of the child. Quite often the parent is frankly puzzled but most often does not understand and therefore refuses to accept that the child is going through phases of growth-experience which the parent has not had. This misunderstanding, in most cases, is caused by the parents' lack of appreciation of the difference in the speed and impetus of our evolutionary consciousness in general as against the speed of evolutionary consciousness when they were themselves at school. This basic ignorance sets in motion a series of psychological neuroses which constantly feeds back to gain force and justification from the maternal and paternal protective instincts which themselves take various forms of emotional expression ranging from nagging the child at home and imposing extra work, to violent attacks on the teachers of the child.

The most powerful justification the parents have is always based on the accepted premise of their love for the child. This of course could take us into the most complicated regions of psychological discussion where we would come at last to the question "What is love?" and we would have to answer either with a positive "God is love" or a negative "Love is whatever can still be betrayed". Neither of these answers, however, could give authority to the possessive love of the parent, mainly because this sort of "love" takes no cognisance of the possibility of Nature's own protection over all growing creatures. Needless to say, a possessive love, which is not really love at all but a bargaining, can have no trust in divine protection because of the anxiety for its own brand of love to be returned or for some kind of gratitude for the expenditure.

Children have to be allowed to grow through experience and the experience can rarely be what the parents would wish. If children are fenced in by "do this", "don't do that", frustrations are born which may last a lifetime or create blocks in the mental being so as to prevent free growth, setting up inhibitions which limit the consciousness to the ordinary, the general, the inartistic, the uncreative, the low and the vulgar.

Parents must learn to put their trust in the Divine Mother, having the faith that the best will happen when they put their chidlren into Her care.

Integral Child Education

SITA RAM JAYASWAL

Sri Aurobindo and the Mother were for such a system of child education as would awaken the dormant psychic mind and develop supramental consciousness.

Sri Aurobindo was fully aware of new educational trends and noted the direction of their movement.
He wrote:

"The discovery that education must be a bringing out of the child's own intellectual and moral capacities to their highest possible value and must be based on the psychology of the child-nature was a step forward towards a more healthy because a more subjective system; but it still fell short because it still regarded him as an object to be handled and moulded by the teacher, to be educated."[1]

Sri Aurobindo further stated:

"But at least there was a glimmering of the realisation that each human being is a self-developing soul and that the business of both parent and teacher is to enable and to help the child to educate himself, to develop his own intellectual, moral, aesthetic and practical capacities and to grow freely as an organic being, not to be kneaded and pressed into form like an inert plastic material."[2]

---

[1] *Integral Education*, Pondicherry: Aditi Karyalaya, Sri Aurobindo Ashram, pp. 35-36.

[2] *Ibid.*, p. 36.

The Child as a Developing Soul

The first important thing to be noted in the context of integral child education is that it is the main responsibility of both parent and teacher to help the child in his self-development and self-education. According to Sri Aurobindo, each human being is a self-developing soul. It is this truth which has been tragically ignored by modern educators and has further led to certain misunderstandings pertaining to education of the child.

The integral child education is based upon the principle that such education should be given to children as would help in their all-round development. The all-round development of the child can take place when due attention is paid to the development of his body, emotions and mind at the first stage. A little later provision must be made for the psychic and spiritual development of the child. Only then educational needs of a self-developing soul can be fulfilled. In this context the following observation of Sri Aurobindo is most significant:

"The fulfilment of the individual is not the utmost development of his egoistic intellect, vital force, physical well-being and the utmost satisfaction of his mental, emotional, physical cravings, but the flowering of the divine in him to its utmost capacity of wisdom, power, love and universality and through this flowering his utmost realisation of all the possible beauty and delight of existence."[1]

Sri Aurobindo desired the flowering of the Divine in the child so that true knowledge could be acquired by him. If the child is given a systematic integral education, he will

[1] *Ibid.*, p. 37.

certainly develop his mind to the extent that he receives the Light, his heart is filled with Love and his whole life is permeated with Power.

It was once enquired from the Mother as to what should be the aim of education and the Mother made the following statement:

> *There is a Divine Reality wanting to be manifested. We aim at knowing this Reality and working for its manifestation.[1]*

Thus it is evident that the integral child education aims at self-knowledge and desires the child to realise the Divine Reality which is within him and manifest it in his thoughts, feelings and actions.

Physical Development of the Child

In integral child education the physical development is given as much importance as the mental development or the development of other aspects of child personality. What is the reason? The reason is that the human body functions as a base (adhara). The physical development is the foundations of all other developments which we desire in the child. Sri Aurobindo has stated:

"In the use of such activities as sports and physical exercises for the education of the individual in childhood and first youth, which should mean the bringing out of his actual and latent possibilities to their fullest development, the means and methods we must use are limited by the

[1] N.C. Dowsett & S.R. Jayaswal (ed.), *The New Approach to Education*, Pondicherry: Sri Aurobindo Society, 1974, p. 29.

nature of the body and its aim must be such relative human perfection of the body's powers and capacities and those of the powers of mind, will, character, action of which it is at once the residence and the instrument so far as these methods can help to develop them."[1]

Thus the purpose of physical education is made clear by Sri Aurobindo. The Mother has given equal attention to the physical development of children. She wrote:

"All education of the body, if it is to be effective, must be rigorous and detailed, foreseeing and methodical. That will be translated into habits: the body is a being of habits. But these should be controlled and disciplined, yet at the same time supple enough to adapt themselves to the circumstances and the needs of the growth and development of the being.

All education of the body should begin at the very birth and continue throughout life: it is never too soon to begin nor too late to continue.

The education of the body has three principal aspects: (1) control and discipline of functions, (2) a total, methodical and harmonious development of all the parts and movements of the body and (3) rectification of defects and deformities, if there are any."[2]

Unfortunately the physical development of children in our schools has been either neglected or given half-hearted attention. In integral child education the physical development of the child has to start from the very beginning so that the child develops a sense of rhythm and

[1] *The Supramental Manifestation*, SABCL, Vol. 16, p. 11.

[2] *Sri Aurobindo and the Mother on Education* (Part I), Pondicherry: Sri Aurobindo Society, 1972, pp. 9-10.

harmony not only in his physical movements but also in self-expression.

Vital Development of the Child

In the integral system of education the term vital has a special significance. In the Yoga of Sri Aurobindo, "The vital is indispensable for the divine or spiritual action – without it there can be no complete expression, no realisation in life.... Without the vital there is no life-force of creation or manifestation; it is a necessary instrument of the spirit for life.... The vital is good when it is properly used; it is a necessary instrument for action."[1]

In common language we are familiar with vitality which is the energy or force within an organism. But here in the context of integral education the vital refers to emotions, passions, etc. All our desires and longings, even love and hate, are the manifestations of the vital in us.

According to the Mother, "Of all education, the education of the vital is perhaps the most important and the most indispensable.... It is of prime importance that the child's education of the vital should begin as early as possible, indeed, as soon as he is able to use his sense organs. In that way, many bad habits would be avoided and harmful influences eliminated."[2]

It is important to bear in mind that the physical development of the child and his vital development are complementary. They support each other. The proper development of the sense organs and other organs is

[1] M.P. Pandit (Comp.), *Dictionary of Sri Aurobindo's Yoga*, Pondicherry: Dipti Publications, Sri Aurobindo Ashram, 1966, p. 195.
[2] *Sri Aurobindo and the Mother on Education* (Part I), p. 11.

intimately connected with the vital development of the child. As a matter of fact the vital development prepares the ground for mental development and the development of character. The Mother writes:

"The education of the vital has two principal aspects. They are very different as to the goal and the process, but both are equally important. The first is to develop and utilise the sense organs, the second is to become conscious and gradually master of one's character....

One must gain a full knowledge of one's character and then acquire control over one's movements so that one may achieve perfect mastery and transformation of all the elements that have to be transformed."[1]

In schools group activities help in the vital development of children. The teaching of arts, music, poetry etc., is essential for the vital development of the child. Human emotions are refined and utilised through music, painting, poetry and drama. In an integral system of education these subjects are given due importance because they are considered necessary for the vital development of the child.

Mental Development of the Child

In modern child psychology mental development is considered very significant because it provides the tools of thinking such as concepts and symbols. The powers of reasoning and logical thinking, memory and imagination are essential aspects of mental development.

In the integral system of education, mental development of the child is considered significant because it

[1] *Ibid.*

72

prepares the child for a higher life. According to the Mother, there are five phases in the mental development of the child. These phases usually appear one after the other. But it may also be seen that these phases occur simultaneously in certain cases. It all depends upon the state and the level of consciousenss of an individual.

The five phases of mental development, as stated by the Mother, are:

"(1) Development of the power of concentration, the capacity of attention.

(2) Development of the capacities of expansion, wideness, complexity and richness.

(3) Organisation of ideas around a central idea or a higher ideal or a supremely luminous idea that will serve as a guide in life.

(4) Thought control, rejection of undesirable thoughts so that one may, in the end, think only what one wants and when one wants.

(5) Development of mental silence, perfect calm and a more and more total receptivity to inspirations coming from the higher regions of the being."[1]

The above five phases of mental development fully explain the significance of mental education in terms of the integral development of the child. If the child develops his power of concentration, the capacity of attention, thought-control, and is able to make his mind silent and calm, only then can we say that his mental development has been satisfactory from the integral point of view.

[1] *Ibid.*, p. 12.

Psychic Development of the Child

In integral child education psychic development occupies the most important place. As a matter of fact the psychic development is the main purpose of integral education. The Mother writes:

"With psychic education we come to the problem of the true motive of life, the reason of our existence upon earth, the very discovery to which life must lead and the result of that discovery, the consecration of the individual to his eternal principle."[1]

In integral child education psychic development may be considered as a high point from which the child is prepared for his spiritual development. In other words, the fundamental problems of life and the world are seen in their true perspective. The child is enabled to look deep into his heart to find the psychic being. In the words of Sri Aurobindo:

"The psychic is the soul or spark of the Divine Fire supporting the individual evolution on the earth and the psychic being is the soul-consciousness developing itself or rather its manifestation from life to life with the mind, vital and body as its instruments until all is ready for the union with the Divine."[2]

Thus the psychic development is actually the development of soul-consciousness. The child is enabled to realise that he is not merely an organism with a body, a vital and a mind only. He is a soul within a human frame aspiring to know its real nature. It is quite evident that an ordinary teacher, who has no idea of integral Yoga, cannot help in

[1] *Ibid.*, p. 13.
[2] *Dictionary of Sri Aurobindo's Yoga*, p. 195.

the psychic development of the child. That is why The Mother has said, "One must be a great Yogi to become a good teacher."

For the psychic development of the child it is essential that he learns to concentrate and meditate. According to Sri Aurobindo, concentration is the fixing of the "consciousness in one place or on one object and in a single condition". In other words, the child must learn to fix his consciousness on one object or in one place so that gradually he prepares the ground for his psychic development.

Meditation is also necessary for the psychic development of the child. The child must learn how to meditate. At this point it must be borne in mind that the process of meditation requires great effort because it is difficult. Hence a teacher in the integral system of education has to be a master of the process of meditation so that he may teach children how to meditate and thereby help the psychic development of children under his care.

The dimensions of integral child education include certain aspects of spiritual and supramental development. Modern educators know very little about spiritual education and supramental education. Due to a wrong conception of secularism even such ideas have been ignored in education as are universal in nature and help in the spiritual development of children. It is our hope that in the near future due attention will be paid to the spiritual development of children.

The integral child education remains incomplete without provision for spiritual development. The child should be enabled to know and realise the unity between himself and the Divine Self. The integral child education goes a step forward and proposes a plan of supramental education for children. What is its nature, how it is given to children, can be understood only by those of us who have sufficient knowledge about the psychic being and have attained a sufficient degree of psychic development.

The Child of the Future

MEDHANANDA

Meet Your Descendant

The time is approaching when the secret or more or less unconscious aspiration of the past for the golden child, the child of truth, will become conscious, manifested as genetic engineering.

What does science say about our descendant? He will be taller than we are, but less massive. If I am white-skinned, then he will be darker, and if I am black-skinned he will be fairer. He will be better educated than we are, even if we have three Ph. Ds. He will have intelligent electronic machines to play with which stimulate him carefully, from the very day he is born, to ever greater feats of daring thought.

When he is four years old he will understand symbolic logic and know everything an insurance appraiser knows about statistics. He will be more at home in the world of abstract thought than our ancestor was in the primeval forest. He will specialise when he is ten, and at fourteen start his post-graduate studies, which he will continue for the rest of his life.

He will never stop studying: it is his way of life as a fully-evolved mental being. He will be much more intelligent than we because he will know exactly what his intelligence is. He will consider it his most precious possession, and will have endless means – genetic, nutritional, chemical – to enhance it, and an environment to stimulate it – things you and I never had. The newspapers and books we read he would consider as much an assault on his intelligence as you would consider a blow on your body.

Not only has he specialised, but within his specialisation there are only forty to sixty other people on earth who are able to udnerstand him. He is in weekly conference with them, via computer and personal television.

His home is managed by a group of specialists with computer services which today we couldn't get even in the best hotels, restaurants or hospitals. Service is commonplace to him, and he makes daily use of it through computer channels. He is also more individualized than we are. He knows better what he likes and what he dislikes, and why.

Because of his high intelligence he is more concerned with the life of mind and the life of the spirit. He likes to meditate for long stretches of time, and as a child learned to make his intuitions as constant as a cascade of lightning. His prayers resemble mathematical formulas, even though he has an infinitely richer vocabulary for expressing spiritual concepts than we have. His spirituality is unique.

He has no inhibitions and no complexes. He knows how to take care of his inner being, and when he meditates he soars off like a rocket into the shining oneness of things.

As he is highly specialised, he is also more dependent on the society in which he lives than we are, but he enjoys it more. He is better intergrated, and because of this integration he lives without fear in a friendly universe. He knows that there is no death, only life everlasting. He is never lonely because he has found his true self. He knows that happiness means enjoying the things around him, and

78

for that he doesn't have to possess them; that true joy is to possess the wholeness of things, the wholeness of himself and the wholeness of the universe – a wholeness which, since his babyhood, he has never left.

Second Genesis

The child of the future is human only in the sense that a giant rocket or radiotelescope or hybrid corn is human. He is the child of a new genesis, the brother of plutonium and of the laser beam, the son of biological enginering.

While man was born into a solid, static universe, the child of the future is at home in an exploding universe built of electromagnetic radiation. Nothing could be more different from man and other raw-nature products like man, than the child $= 1$. Though physically he may in the beginning have a vague resemblance to his 'father', his psychological makeup is totally different.

Nothing here of an Odipus complex, or an inferiority complex. There are no ids or egos in him, neither Narcissus nor superego. And no ancestor or worship either. A clean-cut mutation, away from all his animal inheritance. He is not even what you are to the big apes, though perhaps what you are in comparison to the reptiles. He is the first representative of a new consciousness, non-mammalian just as a computer or an automated factory is non-mammalian. What nature tried in vain to do with us, she will accomplish by biological engineering with him. It is not we with our apish manners, but he who will be the earth representative in deep space. We will be remembered only as his forerunners, just as the *coelacanth* was our forerunner. He sees himself first and foremost as a child of a new consciousness, and not as a descendant of man or of man-consciousness or ego-consciousness – terms he uses to describe us, the opposite of cosmic and solar consciousness which are his ranges. The movements of our consciousness are almost exclusively from outside inward. All our knowledge is superficial, sensory knowledge, acquired outside of ourselves. What we have studied, painfully over twenty-five years, and learned in our primitive, superficial way, he possesses when he is three years old by simply opening himself. He breathes in knowledge as we breathe oxygen, and what we call learning he calls yoga: to become one with. By this yoga he acquires what we call mathematics, chemistry, or medical science, and these things in turn he calls abstracting, concreting and healing. For him they are all basic movements of consciousness.

We have never understood the inside of things. Our psychology is the most chidish of our sciences. We tried to understand the inside of an atom, of an electron, of a proton, and failed. His only science, psychology, is the science of the inside of things: the psychology of a galaxy, the psychology of a sun, down to the psychology of a quark or a nanoquark.

His consciousness is always outgoing, like the rays of the sun, therefore he calls it solar consciousness. We look at things in order to see them, he in order to bless them. We use our hands to take hold of things, he to impose new ranges of consciousness on things.

We fight against nature; we want to conquer it. But all creation obeys him without his even expressing a wish. In the same universe we live in our own hell, and he in a fairy-story paradise. Time – our enemy, our destroyer – together with all the other powers of the universe is his errand boy, his obedient servant. We meet others to profit from them. He meets them to exchange his bliss. Death is our end, but his door to new life.

REFERENCES TO THE ARTICLES REPRODUCED

"Education of the Child", *SABCL*, Vol. 15, pp. 27-28; Vol. 17, pp. 214-15, 222-23, 210-11.

"Teaching Children", *Sri Aurobindo and the Mother on Education* (Part II); Sri Aurobindo Society, 1972, pp. 19-26. *A New Education for a New Consciousness* (Comp.), Sri Aurobindo International Centre of Education, 1992, pp. 123-26, 131-33.

"Children and Child Mentality", *Collected Works of Nolini Kanta Gupta*, Vol. Three, Sri Aurobindo International Centre of Education, 1972, pp. 194-97.

"The Growing Child", *Education and the Aim of Human Life*, Sri Aurobindo International Centre of Education, 1967, pp. 149-155.

"Children: Right Educators", *Lights From Sri Aurobindo*, 1970, pp. 80-84.

"Foundation of the Whole", *Pedagogics of the Kindergarten*, D. Appleton and Company, New York, 1907, pp. 6-13.

"Goal-Forming Activity of the Child", *The Education of Children*, George Allen & Unwin Limited, London, 1957, pp. 5-21.

"The Adult and the Child", *The Secret of Childhood*, Orient Longmans, Bombay, 1961, pp. 3-11.

"The Child of the Future", from the Editorial Board of = *1*, a magazine published by Sri Aurobindo Society, Pondicherry.

Abbreviations used in footnotes and references:

SABCL *for* Sri Aurobindo Birth Centenary Library.

CWM *for* Collected Works of the Mother.